I0474932

The Digital Acquisition Cycle™
For Content Creators

Make Sense of Digital Marketing with The DAC™ Model and Turn Your Content into An Acquisition Machine!

Scott Winterroth

Dedication

I want to dedicate this workbook to you, for the ground zero students just learning about digital and conversion marketing/performance-based marketing. You are my inspiration for designing the DAC Model.

Acknowledgment

I want to thank everyone who contributed to refining my ideas on paper. Writing a book is surely a challenge, one that was made easy by the support of the editorial team that worked night and day with me to bring this book to fruition.

About the Author

Scott Winterroth is blogging coach, podcaster and business consultant. He answers a variety of questions regarding how to build a sustainable ecosystem with content and leverage digital marketing. He wants to emphasize the importance of understanding the tactical aspects of digital marketing, but his students lack a big-picture strategy.

He knows the reality that you can't really start to use a platform like Facebook for strategy until you answer some foundational questions and prepare yourself for a long road ahead.

His workbook outlines a strategy that he has forged from being on the front line and based on his experience deploying successful digital strategy campaigns.

With this book, he is embarking on a journey to give you the knowledge, all compiled in one place that he had to work to get for years. To learn more about Scott, visit his website, scottwinterroth.com.

Preface

This workbook is focused on the DAC Model that can assist anyone in building their digital presence by using simple yet applicable rules. For this purpose, you may or may not have prior experience with sales or marketing or PR. All that matters is your willingness to learn how this model works and how it can help your business flourish. With a resource like this book, you can even start a blog of your own. Whether you have a WordPress website or even if you have a social media website, you can amplify the effect of all your digital endeavors with the DAC Model. This model will help you in turning the traffic to your website into subscribers.

The DAC Model loop product, pre-acquisition, remarketing keeps your business up on its toes over its digital marketing strategy. With this model, you can create, Q&A to help them identify a business plan, marketing plan, and idea roadmap. These plans and strategies allow you a complete business cycle of 90 days for your startup plan.

Content

Introduction

So you have an idea for a blog, and now you need a plan.

Or you're not sure if the existing blogging strategy is working.

You're in the right place. This book was designed to provide you with clarity on how to leverage digital marketing strategy through your blog.

Let's face it; when it comes to blogging and digital marketing, there are a lot of moving parts. Keeping track of everything, from creating content to monitoring paid traffic - it can be enough to make your head spin. Without proper planning or a plan at all, you can easily let things slip and potentially overspend or underperform. It is difficult to manage the entire digital content marketing process, but it can be done when you have a strong understanding of what matters the most.

It's easy to fall into the social marketing trap. When you're just getting started, it's easy to want to test out each platform to see which one is the easiest or the most fun for you. Don't get me wrong - I encourage you to try things out and participate in this process. That is how you test ideas and build a following. But just remember these platforms are not designed in your best interest. No, they want your content and advertising so they can increase their profits – not yours.

Each platform should be used according to its worth to you, not according to what it does for you, as they are each just one small component of a viable online marketing strategy. In this book, we're going to put each social media platform into its proper place within your strategy.

At any given time, it might make sense to jump into a new social platform because it seems to generate action. I want you to stop before you jump and consider how this might affect your strategy and goal attainment. That is the premise of this book; to help you design a digital marketing strategy that puts it all into perspective, so you know when to jump or when to pull out.

This book does not provide tactical information on how to use a particular social network or blogging platform, but rather a big-picture marketing strategy designed for content creators and online entrepreneurs. Over the last 15 years, the internet disrupted marketing and public relations forever. This workbook outlines a strategy that I've forged from being on the front lines. It is based on my experience deploying successful (and some not so successful) digital strategy campaigns.

Today, as a blogging coach, podcaster, and business consultant, I answer a variety of questions regarding how to make money with content, as well as how to leverage digital marketing. It's important to understand the tactical aspects of digital marketing, but I find that many of my students lack a big picture strategy. The truth is, you can't really start to use a platform like Facebook for strategy until you answer some foundational questions and prepare yourself for a long road ahead.

I hope to provide the tools to do exactly that in this book.

Before a single post is published or a photo is snapped; before we get wrapped up in the busy work of blogging and creating content; before all of that, we must first conceptualize the big picture of how everything will gel. It's easy to get wrapped up in posting and generating likes, but it's crucial to determine how it will all coalesce into a coherent strategy.

This book is about the big picture strategy because I believe that anyone looking to profit from online marketing must build a strong visualization about how they will make solid returns on their investment (ROI). The Digital Acquisition Cycle model, as I outline in this book, does exactly that. I've created a model for mapping out your marketing strategy so you can focus on what's important now, and in the future.

It's safe to say that nearly anyone can create a social media profile or blog account and then publish content on these. The harder part is determining how to leverage the right content at the right time for the right audience, and thus turn a profile or blog into a profitable strategy. In 2008, I was that person. I created a blog and social media presence with little to no strategy; I simply followed the instructions and hit submit. Boom, blog launched, business cards printed, and I was the editor-and-chief of a country music blog.

My intent was to have fun and gain respect among the local music scene, and I figured I could determine how I would make money later. As they say, starting is half the battle. I published content to my blog, gained some search engine traction, and gained some respect among the niche community I formed. It was great for a while; it opened many doors for me. But gradually, it all started to become too demanding, and I lost interest. I didn't have the proper monetization plan to sustain my operational costs, and my overall enthusiasm wavered.

That money problem continued to bug me in the back of my mind, like a bad dream. I needed to make money from my blogging efforts to prove to myself and my wife that it was worth the time and effort. Running a high traffic website is not a no-cost proposition - the bills started to mount up, and I needed to justify the time and resources I was sinking into my blog. Bottom line, I wanted people who benefited from the blog to pay up.

I learned that it is easy to gain respect when you show up and produce something of value. But it's much harder to sell something when the intended buyers can't find your value. I couldn't grasp how the followers of my blog were willing to pay hundreds of dollars to see a concert but not willing to pay me a lousy five bucks for a subscription. I failed because I did not yet have the foresight to create a true product offering and a sustainable ecosystem that people wanted and would support and financially participate in.

During my country music blog days, there was a popular song by artist Brad Paisley called *Letters to Me*. The lyrics are about a fictitious letter containing wise advice the artist had written to his younger self. I think we all wish we could give spot advice to our younger selves. If I were somehow able to send that letter to me, my twenty-something-year-old self-starting my blog, it would be this book.

Back then, I had a vision for what I wanted and a short term learn-as-I-failed plan. What I didn't have was the foresight into how I might match a product with what my readers would actually be willing to purchase. I wasn't the only one. Mainstream newspapers and magazines are still trying to figure out this same problem today. I definitely don't have all of the answers, but what I do hope to share with you is a culmination of my own experimentation, wins and downright failures as a blogger, marketer, and entrepreneur. The Digital Acquisition Cycle strategy is the byproduct of my learning by doing. I hope that you can learn from my mistakes. Dubbed the DAC Model for short, this is a strategy that I've identified to help my clients and students find their most profitable marketing objectives and build a simple plan to grow their following and create a sustainable content marketing program.

Not every strategy or promotion is going to be spot on, but what is important is the effort to find that right one. What worked for me might very well not work for you. What I do hope is you can learn my story and use these concepts to make them your own. If anything, I hope this helps you ask the right questions that might just spark that one idea that lands you on the path to success.

You Are Your Marketing Strategy

There is neither an artificial intelligence powered machine blogger nor automatic marketing…yet. As I write this, every strategy requires at least one person behind it, and the skills of that person mean everything to the strategy at hand.

Elevating your skills and digital marketing savvy is vital for selling online and building authority. Digital marketing is almost a sport, where it helps to learn as much about every aspect as possible and practice often to refine your edge. I congratulate you for picking up this book, but I will also be the first to say there's a lot more than simply launching a blog.

Your blog alone, albeit critical, is not your marketing engine. YOU are the marketing engine.

To excel in the *"digital marketing business"* requires a skill that's easy to explain but takes a certain person to actually enact. One must live with a growth mindset and actively seek learning opportunities, even beyond simply enrolling in online courses or workshops.

Seminars and conferences are great wayfinders and can open doors for mentors, research, and creative inspiration. By far, the best learning opportunities come from acting and, in the process, making mistakes.

We live in a consumption friendly society, where it's easy to binge-watch reruns the entire weekend or play video games from dusk until dawn. I know this because I constantly fight the urge to participate in these activities and regret giving in when I haven't completed a post or writing goal. It goes without saying that mindless, unmonitored consumption is kryptonite to the highly productive content creator. To succeed in this game, one must really take charge. Turn off the TV, uninstall that computer game, and start creating a rhythm that generates high-quality content. All of the self-help books and motivational talks in the world can't help if one is not willing to actually take steps to make it happen. This is especially so when the going gets tough, and the pressure is on. Take it from someone who truly understands - just don't quit.

Those who win at the digital marketing game are the ones who seek to continuously generate quality written content, who test powerful ads that generate traffic, and who strategically participate in social media. The more frequently a visitor hits a website, blog or social profiles and sees your offer online, the more likely they'll come around to make a sale, become a follower or participate in your general crazy. I found this out the hard way. It only really started to happen for me when I was willing to take charge, make mistakes, and ready myself for the marathon of marketing.

In this book, I ask rhetorical questions to invoke thought around goals and marketing strategy. Most of these questions spawn from my own self-doubt and general crazy, which I've found I have in common with most content creators and web entrepreneurs. I do stress that no advice is one size fits all. What worked for me may not work for you. My goal is to provide you with a foundation for testing what will become your ticket to success. I challenge you to answer the hard questions, the ones that maybe you've been avoiding or don't want to answer. Stop and ask: why are you doing what you're doing?

If your answer comes down to something like I'm doing this because I want to grow as a professional and I'm willing to put in the time to make it happen, well then, I'm here to help you. I hope you find this book positively challenging and that it gives you a better understanding of a sustainable digital marketing strategy that you can actually use and explain. If you have any questions, feedback or need advice, contact me directly at scott@frontandsocial.com

SCOTT WINTERROTH

How This Book Works

The Digital Acquisition Cycle book is divided into three main parts, with the first part focusing on you and exposing a true purpose. Part two is about audiences and how to reach one. The final part is a dive into the Digital Acquisition Cycle (DAC) Model. I borrow the biblical *"thine"* reference for each chapter heading because living a digital marketing campaign is similar to practicing a religion. You have to believe in something greater than yourself, live the daily teaching, and spread unto others your divine *"marketing"* mission. I'm not saying that what I'm proposing to you in this book should be considered a religion or compared to any religion or belief in particular.

However, if you want to excel at digital marketing, one must live the mission. The first campaign is a lot of work, and it will likely be one of the most taxing endeavors you will ever undertake. You will want to quit almost every day. I highly encourage you to keep it up by measuring your process and celebrating the small wins. These small wins will add up to something great. I guarantee you that when you reach the top, you will realize that it all started with small wins and a big picture plan.

I have ended each chapter with a series of what I call *"anytime questions,"* which I refer to when I need to accelerate, or when I'm in the thick of it and need some creative inspiration to get me out of a rut. There are no right or wrong answers; just use them as a creative exercise to poke about your ideas.

Marketing Myths Debunked

This is a good way to level the playing field for any misconceptions. The following myths are quite common about marketing:

- Marketing is complicated. *(Not really)*
- Marketing and advertising are costly. *(Sometimes)*
- Marketing is only for big businesses. *(Hell no!)*
- Marketing can be automated so I can find a tool that will do everything for me.
- *(You still have to set it up and monitor it often.)*

- I should use X platform because it's where all the users are. *(No – diversify until you have a platform to work from.)*
- Anyone can do social media. *(Yes)*
- Anyone can do social media marketing *(No, it takes true skill.)*
- I can expect immediate results. *(The biggest joke of the century!)*

Part 1
Your Purpose

Know Thyself

Before you engage in a plan or build a product, it's important to first take a moment to reflect on this: *"What am I really trying to do here? What does success look like in these areas? How will success evolve, in six months and in six years?"* I know it's hard to visualize success when you don't really know what you're about to embark on or when you're struggling to simply get to the point that makes sense to you. That's OK.

This is simply a brainstorming activity, so you don't have to tear through all the realms to find an answer to them. These questions will trigger one very basic yet extremely important part of your digital marketing plan. They will help you identify the ultimate purpose that you're chasing and willing to keep running after in the long run!

Sometimes, success is merely defined by you finding the true meaning of success. What I can guarantee is that you won't find it until you try.

With every post published, every problem circumvented, there is a lesson learned.

Welcome to the creative mindset!

When I established my first blog, I had no idea of the ancillary web skills that I would learn along the way. These skills are now highly valuable and in demand by employers. Because I was willing to take the time and figure it out, I was able to acquire something extremely precious within the spectrum of my blog. No one forced me to learn these or told me I would succeed or fail on their basis. Success only came because I was willing to take the time to figure it out and determine what I was really trying to accomplish.

First Question: Who Am I?

There's sometimes a bit of disagreement when it comes to marketing. Some think of marketing as something that can be simply turned on or off, or that it just involves posting to a Facebook page. Both examples are far from reality.

Marketing is more about promoting your business, and it comes in many forms. Digital marketing, on the other hand, is a combination of website development and campaign management. Executing a comprehensive digital marketing strategy can sometimes take a few weeks to several months to get off the ground. Of course, depending on your goals, the size of your team, your budget, and your commitment, this timeline can vary to vast proportions. It's critical to stop for a moment, dig a little deeper within yourself, and determine if you're ready to embark on such a huge commitment.

Are you willing to spend many hours building campaigns, testing new ideas, and creating content that will only provide a return on an investment after you have it dialed in?

The key ingredient to almost any digital marketing campaign is commitment. You need to sustain your online marketing strategy, even when it is difficult. Sustainability is what works for every digital marketer who seeks success. If you can't take the pressure of pulling through the tough times, you can't possibly imagine surviving in this area. That's why many of us set out to create a blog, a new business or marketing strategy, but lose steam when the hard stuff turns passion into procrastination. This is especially so when there's little to no accountability for your success or failures.

Let's face it, you can't always live life in a passion project. Like most marketers, you're probably reading this because you need to generate new opportunities for your business, make money, and probably because your boss doesn't care about your personal mission statement! The truth is, if you don't somehow align your passions and skills into your day-to-day work, then you might be on a serious path to failure.

How does one find their sweet spot when it comes to passion and authority?

In this exercise, I want you to take the time to identify who you really are as a professional and a person, as well as the skills you have honed along the way. There's no right or wrong answer, but if you are ready to do this, then write it down and keep a reminder of why you're doing what you're doing. There's no better motivation than a daily reminder of your *"why,"*

You'll need your why for when you're really going through a tough spot and questioning whether you made the right decisions. This answer will help you stay on the right track.

If you're able to open up and dig deep to determine what you are passionate about, you can happily show up and make it happen every day! You will want to enjoy what you're about to embark on because you will need to spend a lot of hours, maybe even days of your *"spare"* time, researching, crafting content, investing your hard earned money and speaking to anyone who will listen.

Most importantly, you want others to immediately see your passion and relate, so they join you in reaching your goals. Finding your why will help you share your true mission with others. You wouldn't want your efforts wasted just because you couldn't focus on why you do what you do daily.

Most importantly, you will like this process because it's easy to focus on something that you enjoy. If it's your passion, if it entertains you, you will love it beyond anything else. That said, even if something is your passion, it doesn't always turn out to be the best or most profitable profession.

I'm passionate about a lot of things. How does one choose?

You should pick what allows you to live every moment of your experience and makes for a great career at the same time.

For instance, I really enjoy camping. The process of gearing up for the trip, setting up camp, and enjoying a campfire with friends is something that I look forward to.

But could I author a blog about camping?

Probably not. While I do enjoy camping, I'm not an expert or not passionate enough to write about it. Frankly, I don't care enough to write about it or wish to be known as a camping expert.

I also question my ability to monetize that authority because I can't see myself being a trail guide, extreme camp host, or build any type of product. If you're going to invest your time and resources into growing your authority on a particular topic, then you should have a clear cut path to a return on investment. I'm sure my camping blog would fail after about a couple of posts, as I would run out of ideas or simply just stop giving a hoot.

Now, on the flipside, I've worked in the events and meetings industry for over 11 years and have established credibility working for some rather high profile brands. Can I leverage this experience to become known as an industry leader and use my blogging platform to showcase my expertise? In this space, due to my industry knowledge and people who can vouch for me, I have a much higher chance of leveraging authority and could easily hold my own in conversation over a business dinner.

That is where you would think I would want to focus. I should consider it more as it seems to be where I would have the best chance of winning. Alas, I find myself not going down that road either because it's not something that I'm comfortable writing about. If I dig down deeper, I may have other areas of passion that I would prefer to pursue when it comes to content creation.

What I am passionate about is marketing, digital entrepreneurship, and content creation. That's where I feel I can truly thrive by helping others and sharing the knowledge that I have personally earned by making mistakes and generating my own success.

Find passion in an area where you can easily win.

Find a topic or niche that you can truly win at – one that you are proud to be in and willing to become an expert in. Think about a niche or category where you can forge some type of product that you can sell.

Exercise 1

Answer Question #1: Who am I? Where can I easily win?

Not finding anything? Start with what industries you have worked in, who have you worked for that you could leverage, where you have volunteered, what you cared about in school, what problems you have solved, what problems you face and what you are going to do about them, what you do for fun, and what cities you have lived in or visited. Look for people who need your help, see if there are others like them who could use exactly what you have to offer. If you don't have an answer to some or all the above, then get out, make some connections and experience life! What stories could you tell based on those experiences and use that to build your foundational content marketing strategy should be the following question. If you already have an existing business or you're part of a team, then use this same question and reframe it something like this: *"Who am I within this team or in this organization?"*

What passions can I bring to this team, and how can the team leverage me in the best way possible? Where I will thrive and where will the entire organization thrive because of me? This is truly important if you are the leader of a team.

As an example, here's my *"why"* that I have defined for myself: I want to help others get into content because I have found that blogging and content marketing have helped me in living a more fulfilling life by keeping me in a constant creative mindset. Plus, the ideas and products built from content will go beyond just me and possibly live beyond me.

This is my guiding light, among other more personal endeavors. When you're able to spell out your *"why,"* your mission, and the reason why you enjoy what you're doing, then you will be amazed at how much clarity it will bring to everything you do and what you shouldn't be doing.

What Are We Trying to Accomplish Here?

What's your plan? Digital marketing is a strategy, and it's good to identify a plan, especially before resources are invested in any type of advertising or marketing. Consider what your primary metrics – or Key Performance Indicators (KPIs) are going to be along your journey.

A common basic marketing KPI would be something such as additional revenue generated from a certain amount of marketing dollars spent. It is a good fit for saleable products and services. For example, in Q1, we earned $20,000 with no marketing. In Q2, we spent $15,000 in marketing and generated $200,000 in sales. Therefore, our investment in marketing generated a 100% increase in sales. In this type of campaign, with digital marketing, we can almost granularly see how well our campaign is performing based on what ads and platforms are driving the best conversions.

The web and digital marketing have opened doors to a new type of marketing strategy. The goal is to generate authority, reputation, and brand recognition by offering value-rich content and maybe even without selling an actual product. A KPI for this type of campaign might be to increase the number of email subscribers or grow our number of video views. It's much harder to measure, but when done correctly, *"community building"* is a highly effective long-term strategy for selling multiple products and services which is the ideal strategy for a blogger and content creator.

A savvy marketer is doing a bit of both - advertising and community building – but it's ideal for identifying if your campaign performance should be measured on the number of products sold or the growth of your online community. You decide.

Exercise 1

Answer Question #2: Are we selling a product or selling you?

I recommend creating a clear metric to identify what you're striving to accomplish. For example, are my prospects customers of a product or readers of information?

If you can't decide, then hop back to question one and decide your why. If these answers are not yet clear to you, then you have some homework to do.

Who Are My Ideal Readers?

Every business essentially has a core client base and ideal client. I believe in reaching clients who can best relate to you and what you have to offer. How you relate to an ideal client base may differ on various levels. For example, some clients may like you simply because you feel similar to them. Others may be attracted to your product because it can help them in a new way.

Exercise 1

Answer Question #3: Who are your ideal readers, and how are they similar or different to you. Are they different than who is in your follower database today?

You don't have to be a clone of your ideal client; that is not what I'm trying to get at. What is important is that you understand the people you do business with, and follow or refer to people who are similar to them.

There's a level of built-in trust when we do business with people we can relate to. If you're not the same mold as your ideal clients, then what are some ways you could relate to them and gain their trust?

The beauty of content marketing is we can speak directly to our target audience and share relatable stories that drive trust. Understanding your target audience's needs and pains is paramount to a successful content marketing strategy. When you generally know what their needs and pains are, you can broadcast content that almost speaks directly to their individual desires.

More on this in the audience identification section.

Keep reading!

Expanded Anytime Questions for Part 1

- What are the goals for my digital marketing campaign?
- This month, quarter, year…
- How will I make money? Which avenue is the most profitable?
- What would be the core thing we want a customer/user to do once they learn about our offering?
- Who will likely find the most value in my offering?
- How much *"runway"* do we have to make this campaign to *"take off"*? 1 month, 6 months, 1 year?
- What type of success have we had in the past?
- Why do my clients see value in what I/we am/are offering?
- How much revenue/sales/leads do I expect to make from this campaign?
- What do I want to be known as?
- If I only had 30 seconds to explain who we are or my product, what would I say?
- What do I/we suck at?
- When someone visits my website, regardless of where or how they got there, what and how do

I/we label them? Are they prospects? Leads? Subscribers? Followers? Users?

- Where can you easily be seen as an authority based on who you're associated with and given your previous experiences?
- What makes you happy?

Part 2
Your Offering

If there's anything I've learned from blogging and selling online, it's that it's really hard to sell something if you haven't defined what that product is and who will want it. Reading this here right now may seem like a no brainer. However, when you're actually doing it, you tend to overlook this fact. A clear product offering can turn a hobbyist blogger into a profitable online entrepreneur. To clarify, for the purposes of this book, the term *"product"* often represents a physical thing, something that you can pick up and hold. I'm loosely using the term product to represent basically anything a buyer will pay something of value for. In exchange for this value, the seller provides something tangible (product!).

In reality, a product, in my opinion, might not even be something for sale. Rather a product could equal the sum of someone's program or ideas. Your *"product"* could simply be you selling yourself, maybe as a consultant or even an entertainer. When it comes to blogging and content marketing, the product is often both your content and your audience – depending on who you're selling it to. Regardless of whether your product is a physical thing, a service, or an idea of yours, it must match the consumers' needs and desires.

If You're Blogging, What Is Your Product?

At a very high level, you could consider the author behind a blog as the product. The value proposition for the reader is they like what the blogger has to say, and they come back to patron the blog because of that. The value proposition for the creator is to publish enough content to build an audience and grow their following.

Most bloggers, at some point, want to monetize that effort because let's face it - blogging requires a lot of time to generate traction. The blogger decides to sell advertising. All of a sudden, the product dynamic changes, and now the readership and community surrounding the blog have become a product. Advertisers are paying the blog to promote their product in exchange for access to the blogger's community. This is what's called a two-sided marketplace, where the blogger is responsible for connecting advertisers with readers. Think about that for a second. That's a pretty important responsibility. If an advertiser is willing to pay to advertise on a blog, then there is a level of expectation the advertiser will receive a return on investment for their ad spend to you. Hopefully, double or triple of what they spent in advertising translates into product sales. Some bloggers are able to provide that level, if not more, of return to their advertisers. If you're just getting started or you're not quite a household name yet, then you should deeply consider whether advertising sales are right for your blog business.

There's nothing wrong with reconsidering your options. In digital marketing, sometimes things just don't work out for you, no matter how well equipped you are with your skill set. You can't always control consumer behavior. And if your advertisementdon't sell, then businesses wouldn't want your affiliations. Third party advertisers and marketers are probably not going to have the best interest of your community in mind. Let's face it; they only have the best interest of themselves and the profits of their business.

Could you blame them?

The problem is, online communities and followers are finicky. They want to hear from you.

They have their trust in you only if your message resonates with them. When they start to sense that your message is being diluted by profits, they lose trust interest in what you have to say to them. The last thing you want is to lose the community that you invested your time and resources to build and worked very hard to maintain.

When you start pitching third party products and services, you can very quickly start to dilute your brand's message. Not to mention that sometimes known associations go bad quickly. I'm thinking of a particular sandwich shop pitchman. If you build your audience and also have a product for your audience to purchase, then you don't necessarily need to rely on 3rd party advertisers to profit from. You can profit off your own products and services and potentially keep a much higher profit margin for yourself!

Informational Products

The best products to promote are the ones that you own and control. Some of the products that sell well include online courses, e-books, offline and online events, and other digital products that could support your blogging efforts. Since you're already in the business of creating content, informational products such as eBooks, courses, and online events might already be in your wheelhouse and something that you can turn into a profitable product as you build rapport with your following. Informational products can be fun to create. More importantly, they provide value to your target audience because they are instructional, and often expressed in a voice and medium that your readers are already familiar with. Plus they can generate very valuable feedback from your following.

Once you've identified what your core product is and the audience you're trying to reach, it's much easier to come up with content ideas that will both reach your target and convert them into your product. If you're bootstrapping your efforts, then the revenue generated from these products can be the foundation of something even more sophisticated such as an app or a new business venture. The internet provides a vast platform to sell all kinds of products and services. Everything from coaching to e-learning and freelance services is available on the internet. Your job is to get readers into your marketing funnel so you can sell your products to them.

The rest of this section is about building a deeper understanding of your core product, so when you're in front of your ideal audience, you know exactly what they want and need. When you really understand your audience, you can mold your product around their needs. When that happens, success is almost certain for your business model. This section is divided into two parts, know thy product and know thy audience. They are equally important, and in a perfect world, you would first know your audience and then define your product. However, you and I just don't live in that perfect world. We thrive amid imperfections, and we learn in chaos. Although the following sequence of sections may not be chaotic, it is certainly unconventional. We will now discuss 'know thy product' before we can move on to 'know thy audience.'

Part 2A

Know Thy Product

Let's begin with identifying a core *"product."* As mentioned earlier in this book, when it comes to marketing a product refers to anything, from a physical product or service to a cause or belief. The first order of business is to fine-tune your offering to expose its true value to your audience and demonstrate why they should care about it. Use the first question in this section to find that *"nugget"* of why your product is the right choice among a sea of competition.

Exercise 2

Answer Question #1: What is my product offering? What are we trying to sell, and why are we different?

Dig deep and really find the core of your product offering. It can be difficult to identify a product that people want in a way you can easily create. Start small and work your way towards something more sophisticated.

Exercise 2

Answer Question #2: What are the benefits of our offering? What are the features?

When determining how you are going to present your product, it's ideal for determining its true benefit to your users. For example, by taking this course, I will help you save time and produce a higher quality of work. That is a benefit that someone will receive by taking the course you are offering. Instead of focusing on a particular feature of the product that may not guarantee its sale, you should focus on exactly what this product can do for the audience.

For instance, you could say that the course comprises of 20 videos, each of which is an hour long. But while this is a feature of the course, it doesn't guarantee any subscription to the course. It's nice to know about this feature, but it doesn't sell me on why I would want to watch these videos.

Exercise 2

Answer Question #3: Where are my entry points? How are we going to market this to *"prospects"*? What are they willing to pay and what will we give them in return?

Your product likely has only a few entry points. For example, a free trial or a sample lesson, or a free chapter can be an entry point for the course you are offering. These are marketing tools that you can leverage to grow likeability among your audience. If you can build your reputation among your targets, then they will be more likely to purchase the full program or make a recommendation to a friend to buy the course. Can you offer a trial period, a money-back guarantee, or something else that reduces the stress on the buyer but also gets your foot through the door?

What are some of the ways you can help reduce friction among prospective buyers?

Just make sure to live up to your promises!

Part 2: Expanded Anytime Questions

- What type of readers do I not want?
- How will prospects pay for this product?
- If a prospect were to learn one thing about our offering, what would that key benefit be?
- What do I wish my prospects knew about me, my product/services?
- How demonstrable is this product?
- What would an ROI positive campaign look like?
- How long can I expect my customer to use my product or service?
- Should I use pricing and promotional strategy?
- How can we incorporate exclusivity and lock users into our product?
- What type of support questions do we receive?
- What feedback and feature requests have we received?
- What is the risk/reward for this campaign strategy?
- What might be some frequently asked questions that our average user might have?
- What is my budget to test, to accelerate?
- What would 5 new sales bring to this budget?

Section Bonus Activity: User Testing & Feedback

Read your own blogs and make sure to scrutinize your product yourself. Watch your own marketing emails come in and see if they are too aggressive or too passive at any points. Take this to the next level and enlist friends, family members or even clients who are not biased and will give you their honest opinion. Ask them to review your offering before it goes live to the rest of the world

Part 2B

Know Thy Audience

What keeps them up at night?

For this section, I want you to think of a few people you know personally who are the ideal users of your product or service. Why would they want to use your product? If you can, ask them this. Shape your offering around that user and their feedback.

Exercise 2

Answer Question #4: How are you going to reach people who know nothing about you or your product?

What type of marketing, advertising, and PR strategies are you going to deploy to reach people that fit your target audience?

For example, let's say we're going to use Facebook Ads and focus on targeted geographic areas of Chicago to users within a certain age group. Maybe your blog is about gardening tips so we would want to target homeowners with a large yard to garden.

Let's dial into the basics of audience identification. Start mapping out where your ideal customers live and work. Determine their level of education, employer, age, marital status, and other demographic details.

Exercise 2

Answer Question #5: What is the entire lifecycle of a follower/client?

This question is harder, but I want you to map out the entire ecosystem of your product, from when the prospect just learns about your blog to the path for becoming a 1st-time client, and beyond.

What are their needs along the journey, and how does this change as they move farther along your ideal customer journey? In the very beginning, your prospect will require information that entices them to make a purchasing decision. After they become a customer, they will then have an entirely new set of needs, from help tutorials to tactics that minimize buyer remorse. Determine what type of content and voice will follow your users along their journey and map out what will go when.

Example User Journey

Prospect: A prospect is an ideal client that we haven't yet reached, but who we are trying to create initial awareness in through marketing and advertising. A prospect is essentially a guess, someone we think would have an interest in our product and the resources to acquire it.

Lead/Subscriber: A lead is someone who has expressed interest in what we have to offer and requires follow-up marketing to make the final decision. For example, a lead may be someone who has left behind information on our website, or called to inquire about our product. In content marketing, a subscriber can also be a lead because we have their email address and are able to continue to ship more content to them.

Client/User: A client or user is someone who is fully invested in our product. They have crossed the line by making a purchase, and in exchange, we have delivered something of value to them.

Advocate: An advocate is a satisfied client who is willing to provide positive feedback to either the product owner or other prospects who then become leads.

Part 2: Expanded Anytime Questions

- What would keep your audience engaged?
- What level of immediacy will my audience have with this product? Will they even know they need it at all?
- What is the value in this for my reader?
- Who are my early adopters, mass-market user? How does your value change based on the type of user? What level of product education will be involved?
- Out of all of my prospect types, which ones are likely easiest to reach, and the best fit for me? Which one will be most receptive to me, my style, and my offering?
- If you're trying to sell to corporate execs, but you're running around in shorts and long hair, will they be receptive to you?
- If your blog is really cute, how will your audience respond to that?
- What demographic/geographic would provide me the most value and create a long-term client?
- What does a cold prospect look like?
- What does a warm prospect look like?

- How big is this audience? If I had 10% of this audience pay for my product, how much revenue would that be?
- Acquisition
- What types of websites/organizations would make great inbound links to my site?
- Who might be power partners to refer to my funnel?
- Where does my audience consume other information?
- Social networks
- Websites
- Organizations
- Television and radio
- Influencers they follow
- What needs does my target audience have?
- Are these needs they recognize?
- What stage of the need process are they at?
- What type of questions will my target audience have about my product offering?
- What type of web searches would my target audience make on average?
- What types of stories/information could I share/create that they would find or spark their interest?
- What type of web traffic do we receive now? Is this ideal for what we want?

- Suggestions: Make sure Google Analytics Demographic tracking is enabled
- What would make a solid and memorable impression on your prospect? Is there something that will spark their needs with a visual cue? One time, I brought umbrellas to a networking meeting because I'm their web rainmaker.
- What type of content, platforms would my audience be most receptive too?
- What type of activities or events can you create to better learn about your customer base or target prospect?
- After they purchase this item, what type of challenges might they be fearing? How can I combat them from experiencing buyer's remorse? How can I transition/onboard them best from prospect to user?
- Who might be influential to them, and who might they aspire to?

Section Bonus Activity: Audience Research

If I could pick anywhere in the world at any moment to shoot up a road flare that points people to a large billboard, where and when would you do that?

Go on Twitter, Instagram, LinkedIn, or Facebook and pull the profiles of three to five current customers or ideal customers. Use these profiles to find like-minded people who would also find value in your product. Print them out and put them on your wall as these are the people you are writing for and marketing to.

Part 2 Summary

Are you trying to sell something people need and are aware of today, or is it something they might need after some education? Explain why is so. Sometimes you're just too far ahead of the curve. Pick something that will work today and build towards market adoption.

Part 3
The DAC Model

How the heck do you get people to find you online? If you're thinking about launching a blog or you've already got one up, you probably as some level wondering how are you going to generate traffic. You're not alone; that's the million dollar question. If you've already built a blog, or maybe even a product, you're off to a good start. If you're at this point, you might be thinking. What's the next thing I probably need to do to get traffic? Logically, you might just start posting blog content and work on social media engagement. Because that's what bloggers do, right?

Writing and posting content is definitely a great place to start if you don't really have a plan. But when it comes to leveraging blogging to its full potential, posting content is only half of the equation. Let me share with you a plan that I have designed to help you really launch your blog into a legit growth strategy. You can write and publish content until you're blue in the face. Go for it, but if you want a plan that allows you to measure your success and actually make money online, then please keep reading and pay close attention. First, let me say this. If you plan to blog just because it's a creative outlet for yourself and you're not interested in building an online empire, put this book down now and go blog. I, for sure, don't judge. If blogging content on your own path is best for you, then do what generates the most happiness for yourself.

But if you want to get seriously entrepreneurial about your blog's strategy and potentially make money from your efforts, keep reading. I know, I know. Making money from blogging, in some circles, is a dirty phrase, often used by snake oil salesman. I'm way more pragmatic. I'm sharing examples of campaigns that I have personally deployed and test. In this book, I will share with you in my strategy for making money through blogging. I'm not going to promise you that you will make a boatload of money, or that it will be easy and you can do it from the beach or something. Heck, you might even lose money before you realize what you've just done. Blogging is hard work, often taken for granted by readers. To do it right requires a perfect combination of risk-taking, fearless content creation, and luck. Heck, it takes a certain type of person to even launch a blog, let alone create content. Blogging often comes down to: do you want to make an investment and take a risk on yourself? Creating content and marketing your content requires a lot of work. Not to mention the fear of putting something out into the world. Your commitment to your blog is the same as if you were to open a physical new store - you must show up every day to open and close the store. No one else will do it for you. Only you can do it. If you were a small business owner with a retail store and you didn't show up to open the store, it would be easy to figure out why your business is failing.

Similarly, many creators set out to grow and profit from blogging, but they don't show up every day to create and publish content. There are a million excuses why; I've had many myself. But let's face it – if you don't create, you can't grow. I think one major reason why people's attention towards their blog wavers is because there's no immediate return on their time investment, or they don't even have a clear business plan for how they will make money from their efforts.

Let's face it - blogging is damn hard. If you want to become known online, you must look at a blog as not simply a website, but one part of a larger sales strategy where you actually recoup your time investment into creating content. Let's say you started to generate $5,000 a month from your blog. Would that help keep your attention and focus? It would for me! Don't think of blogging as just a place to post content; rather let me share with you a sustainable ecosystem that includes acquiring visibility online and turning users into paying customers.

That's what we will explore the rest of this book. How you build a user acquisition system so you can grow your visibility and generate revenue that you can use to either pay yourself or reinvest in your business' growth. In addition to my own wins and losses, I've watched and even helped many other bloggers and startups grow and flounder over the years. From 2012 to 2018, I created and hosted a local event called Bloggers Meet Startups. This was my signature pitch event, and it was well-received by the local community. It was a fun and creative way for founders and bloggers to connect and forge business collaborations. We made plenty of successful connections, such as linking travel startups with travel bloggers, lifestyle bloggers with fashion startups, and food bloggers with restaurants. It was a great time and a fun way for startups to generate some publicity and build relationships. To my surprise, I later found out that we even matched a future husband and wife! These grassroots events were a great way to bring value to my community and create exposure for my business for little to no cost. I've also watched some of the blogs that participated eventually fizzle out. This insight made me realize the true pitfalls with blogging. It is one reason why I wanted to write this book; I want all bloggers who are just getting started to understand the work required if you want to build something of substance.

It's safe to say that nothing is total failure. There's always a deep learning experience that comes from trying. In fact, most true successes in life are generally on the back of failure. The one thing the successful bloggers had in common was their ability to blur the lines between a blog and a business startup by creating a product or service that people actually want. Out of the gate, they had a sustainable ecosystem for elevating their blog into a content marketing machine.

Once you identify a product, as we explored in part 2, you must match that with a target audience. Then your content creation strategy of what posts to create will immediately become clear. Your content will center on driving users to your product offering. If you don't have a central purpose or a clear product offering, then you are likely setting yourself up for failure. The blogs that failed, including some of my own, failed after the bloggers realized the amount of effort and resources required to sustain a blog that doesn't really have a true product.

If there's one thing I want to convey with this book, it's that blogging and building a following online alone is NOT a marketing strategy. Blogging can be a great way to build an online arsenal of content, but it is only one part of a larger marketing strategy. No matter how awesome your posts or how often you publish, it won't do a thing until you get real and start to look at your blog as one part of a larger marketing plan. There are a million tutorials and advice on how long or how often you should post. The truth is, no one can really tell you how often to blog or what type of content is best to share and when. Heck, you could write just one blog post that leads prospects to your online product. Promote that one post on Facebook Ads and make a boatload of money with a single blog post. It doesn't often happen that way, but technically it could. What matters is the recipe, you, your content, and your offer.

Anything can happen if you have faith in your product, create valuable content, and live by a plan that allows you to make educated decisions, and take calculated risks. Mediocre bloggers might be solid at regularly creating content, maybe even on a daily basis. But what would take them to go from good to great? Probably a real plan for promoting their work and funneling users into their product. This is where I want to help! As a creator and online entrepreneur, you must always be on the lookout for opportunities to drive traffic and make money so you can sustain your efforts and enthusiasm. You may think that you are not in this for the money. I can understand. I wasn't either when I was blogging in 2008 about my country music community. Let me tell you it wasn't my enthusiasm that drove my blog into the ground. It became burdensome when the website hosting bills ballooned, and I had to decide if the time commitment to creating something that was costing me a significant amount of money was worth it.

I didn't really have a plan in place for how I was going to monetize my efforts. I needed a true product that people would want to pay for and me to profit.

It comes down to you deciding what your true mission is with your blog and your ultimate performance indicators. You are the only person that can determine and create your success. A few years ago, it was ok to just build a blog and get random *"traffic,"* and that was cool. It was considered successful if you could say, *"I have 10,000 visitors a day."* Today, it's challenging to make any type of real money with blog ads. Back then, large amounts of traffic worked for bloggers because a primary source of revenue came from display ads on platforms like Google AdSense – now Google Ads. Site owners were paid by showing ads in bulk. Like most good things, the spammers and gamblers ruined that for everyone. Now AdSense pays pennies per thousands of impressions. Making it near impossible to earn anything worth your time with ad networks.

The best way to quantify and build a true return on investment with your blog is by growing an authority platform where you build a celebrity-like relationship with your following. So if you make a product endorsement on your blog, it will actually drive sales. This is why niche audience targeting and product fit are so important today. If you want to be a celebrity to your following, you will have to find the smallest viable audience that will rally around your shared interest.

Blogging and content marketing today is a two-way communication channel. For years, you could just post blog posts, and that was all you have to do: pontificating to the web and not really engaging a community. Today, it requires you to post content, capture email addresses, and then send email content to your subscribers. Your ultimate goal as a blogger is to convert the right type of visitors into an email database. This might sound cliché, but after you launch a blog, there are only two types of people in the world: those who are on your email list and those who are not. Make it your primary goal to grow your email list following list growth metric. This is your key to starting success.

Email is where you will be able to facilitate stronger relationships with your following while working them over until they are comfortable enough to make a larger purchase from you. The only blog metric that I really care about is the ability to sell a product through the site's email database or something similar. Tell me you have 100,000 Instagram followers, and I'll ask you how useful that is. I will ask you how much revenue have you generated from that. Tell me that you have 5,000 email addresses in your MailChimp account and you sold $150,000 in your online course to that relatively small list with a product that costs less than \$50. That's way more impressive.

Collecting followers on platforms like Instagram, Twitter, LinkedIn, and YouTube - is just like posting content to your blog without promoting it. It is just one part of the digital marketing equation. It's not the only part. The scary part about these popular platforms is that the followers you attract are not yours. It wasn't that long ago that when you posted something to a Facebook Business profile, your users would see it for free. Today, you're almost always required to pay to boost your content if you want more than 10% of your following to see it. That doesn't mean we can't leverage these platforms. Let's just do what we can to diversify your following by collecting emails into your blog's database. It's just too risky to go all in on just one platform. But remember, it's even more of a loss to do nothing and lose all opportunity without trying.

My model, the Digital Acquisition Cycle, is a plan for how you can build independence from the big pay-for-play platforms and leverage a self-hosted blog that you have 100% ownership and control over.

You may be wondering, with all of these big and easy to use social networks, why would you even need a blog or website? That's what the big platforms what you to think. Because they make money from your participation. Your own website is the only thing you really can control and own. When it makes sense, we want to filter users off of platforms like Facebook, YouTube, and Instagram and send them to our blog, preferably, a self-hosted WordPress blog found at wordpress.org.

This is where you will proudly sell your products and collect email addresses.

Your Prospects and Your Product

In the web business, the user journey is the process of someone using your website. A journey ends when a user finds and completes the intended goal; this is called the conversion. A content strategist maps out each intended step a user should take as they traverse a site and reach various endpoints. This planning process is highly important for information-heavy websites, especially blogs where you have multiple points of entry and, sometimes, exits.

User journey mapping is especially helpful for conceptualizing granular intentions for each user who visits your website. For example, once they land on the homepage, what would ideally be the next step? Or if they find your site through a search-friendly blog post, what would we want them to do next?

I'm sure you've had experience using poorly designed websites or blogs. It's frustrating when information is not organized, or a web interface element does not function properly. There's a good reason it had become a growing industry trend to hire someone to organize your site's content or design an interactive user interface. As the web becomes more and more information-heavy, we must work towards providing the best user experience if we want to stand out among our competition and keep a user's attention for more than a few milliseconds.

Just like building a house or an entire community of homes, it's ideal to architect the intended user interactions before breaking any ground or pouring cement into the foundations. Well-designed properties create effortless user experiences that, when done correctly, can improve sales and engagement, or quality of life in our real estate example. This architecture of a user journey transcends many aspects of design and information architecture, and it's likely that you're the subject of design marketing every day.

- Shopping malls are optimized to drive the most foot traffic to the highest paying retail spaces.
- Grocery store product placement is rated by customer eyesight levels on the shelf with the most profitable products placed at eye level.
- Trade show floors are mapped by foot traffic, and the exhibitors who are most willing to spend the most are sold the highest trafficked areas.

A well-optimized experience pays off.

Much like the real world examples above, we work to optimize our website and blogs for user conversion. For example, once users land on our website for the first time, we use data to examine how they interact with the website to see if they follow our *"bait"* and onto our intended path to the offer. Hopefully, they will land on the offer page where we know we have our best, most optimized content designed to draw the prospects' attention by building upon their interests and desire. The final step is to empower the visitor to take action and become a qualified lead or purchase. For many writers and bloggers, some common examples of call to action can include a book purchase, an online course enrollment or some type of free PDF lead magnet – anything with a value proposition that would lead to a user willingly trading their contact information in exchange.

This is why blogging is such a powerful tool. Not only are we able to build a library of content that is indexed by search engines and easily shareable on social media, but with storytelling and content, we can develop likeability and trust in prospects before they even become a customer. What can ruin a perfectly designed campaign is an outdated website or one that does not play well on mobile devices. This is a quick way to lose momentum. The first order of business is to always modernize your website to provide a fresh experience that feels legit.

Think about it. If you walk into a deli, bar or clothing boutique and it looks like nothing has been updated since the 1990s, what's the first thing you will think? Probably something along the lines of either *"Let's get the heck out of here!"* or *"Well, it should be cheap because they obviously don't invest in their appearance."*

First impressions matter on the web, just like they do in the real world. Make sure your blog represents who you are, and communicates how you can help your prospects. When you walk into a restaurant or establishment that is modern, clean, and welcoming, you become more confident that your money is going to pay for a good experience. You may even be willing to stay longer and pay more if the vibe is just right. Same goes for your website.

Your website content and copy is a critical part of the process. How you portray yourself with video, audio, photos, and copy can make or break your user's experience, trust, and perception. Invest in your website and content – this is your selling tool. This is yet another reason why you need to make money from your blogging endeavors. You will need to reinvest that money into building a better blog, acquiring other websites, or hiring professionals and coaches.

How Do We Drive Traffic to Our Blog?

To properly identify your conversion optimization goals, you must first identify your product's offering. Then, match that with an advertising and PR strategy that will drive users to your website and send them down your funnel and into your buy now page. Building an optimized experience is tricky. It will require failure and testing to become its best version. You've got to get people to your website to see if our optimized design is even working.

Now that we've built it, how will you get visitors to your blog? How do you build awareness, so they know you exist?

The process of optimizing a website blog is important, and we will cover this in more detail as we look further into the conversion. But before we get any further, let's discuss how we're going to build general awareness for your existence and get people to your blog.

Introduction to the DAC Model

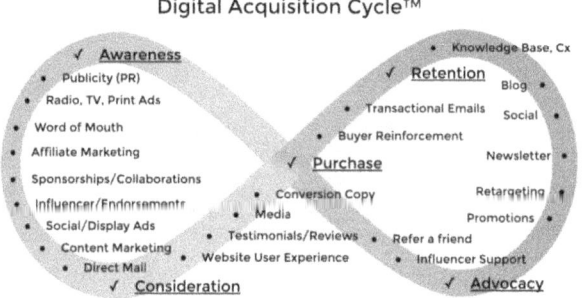

Digital Acquisition Cycle™

From building a country music blog to growing my online consulting and training business and working with some pretty awesome clients and collaborators, I've put in the time to really make some valuable mistakes. I've tried everything at some point to see what works and what doesn't. I've watched strategies change in an instant with an algorithm update. I've dabbled with many emerging platforms and strategies just to try to get some decent results without spending a lot of money. I've seen how the web has become increasingly crowded, harder to game, and upped its pay-for-play when you're a brand.

There's one thing that I feel has been rather consistent across the last two decades when it comes to marketing online, and that is content creation. Creating high-quality content that provides value to a reader is the only consistent strategy. The platforms and techniques may change, but the idea of a self-hosted blog is still a solid strategy. Blogging has its own misconceptions. There's still a stigma that if you're blogging, you can expect tons of free traffic from search and social engines. This is partially true, but it's only if you know how to do it right and have the right mix of content and promotional strategies that you can generate free traffic.

That was then. Today, it's not as easy – especially if you're just getting started. Competition from social networks that now control both eyeballs and advertisers has led to the creation of addictive walled platforms designed to keep users trapped within this ad casino. This has created new problems for independent bloggers who are not looking to give their content away for free to these social networks - or play by their rules. There are other ways to generate visibility for your blog content, but it will likely be with advertising dollars; at least, that's how it will be in the interim, while you begin to seed your own platform. It's scary to spend your hard earned money on advertising or marketing when you're not really sure if or how you might recoup your investment.

Advertising has a reputation for being expensive and reserved for something big brands do to dominate their market. That's not entirely true anymore. Social media and search engine advertising have disrupted the advertising business by introducing a whole new playing field for a relatively low cost of entry. Facebook and Google both offer auction-based, pay-per-click, or pay-per-impression campaigns that allow users to get started with relatively modest budgets. These allow advertisers to pay as little as a few dollars per day.

The difference between these self-serve pay-per-play platforms and what some consider traditional advertising is that digital allows for far greater flexibility as well as the ability to monitor performance in real time. They let advertisers make campaign level adjustments even as dollars are spent, and users begin to interact. This provides an intuitive way to see exactly how your advertising dollars are working for you. If you spend $800 in one month and you generated $10,000 in sales, you can pinpoint with great precision your best performing ads and acquisition channels. Not to mention, you spend next to nothing to build and test advertising creatives.

Digital advertising has become the go-to for small business and startups due to its flexibility and low barrier of entry. That's no wonder, given that a lot of new businesses today are web-based. In comparison to advertising in print, radio, billboard, or television, these more traditional mediums are much more expensive. Creating an ad spot and then paying for available inventory to show your ad can cost thousands of dollars, although of course, it depends on the market and the time your ads will air. Once the order is placed, there are often little to no changes allowed. That doesn't mean traditional advertising doesn't have a place in your marketing strategy. It's just probably not where you will spend your first $50,000 in ad dollars.

Before you go and spend money on advertising, you need a plan. You need to determine what platforms are the best fit for your budget and how you are going to recoup your time and monetary investment. In addition to advertising, there's a whole litany of organic or free marketing opportunity you can deploy to build awareness for your product. By podcasting, creating search engine-friendly content, engaging in social media activity, and utilizing offline opportunities like networking, you can drive awareness. But these activities often can take months to years to gel and require a lot of commitment to execute them well. Where do you start, and what will work best? If you're just getting into the game today, it's unlikely that you will be able to forge ahead without some type of advertising spend. What worked a few years ago - free social media advertising - is gone. Now public companies on Wall Street, platforms like Facebook, Instagram, and Google are looking to profit from your success.

In some ways, free social media and search engine advertising may have done a disservice to your efforts in the past. Fluttering around and creating social media content can be fun, but it's often hard to measure its effectiveness. Digital advertising, while it does cost money, makes it easy to see if it's actually working for you and if you have the proper channels in place. Plus, you can make changes to your strategy in as little as a few days rather than waiting months to years for free organic traffic.

Platforms like Facebook, Google, LinkedIn, and the like make it easy for almost anyone to advertise, that doesn't mean that you should go to these platforms without a plan to follow. That is where the Digital Acquisition Cycle can help.

The DAC Model outlines your most important steps and provides you with a roadmap on how to measure your success and profit from your product using conversion marketing.

Conversion Marketing

In conversion marketing, the objective of the strategy to measure direct outcomes. Since websites and online advertising are rather trackable, your blog will not only serve as your product but as your data source. Therefore you can track outcomes like website registrations, contact form leads, or e-commerce sales.

Before the concept of conversion marketing – or conversion tracking – traditional advertising, marketing, and PR campaigns tended to focus on measuring total estimated reach against sales generation. This was often done with grossly overestimated numbers such as total newspaper distribution or estimated television viewers. In short, you didn't really know what you were paying for, and it was a huge gamble to test something out.

With conversion strategy, a marketer funnels user through a series of steps that lead prospects towards a call to action. This is one of the most intriguing and powerful sales marketing tools today. Conversion marketing allows for data backed decisions, as you learn how users interact with your content and your offer. This model is loosely represented by the common household funnel that starts as a wide capture basin top and shrinks down into a narrow pipe spout at the bottom. It is a metaphorical representation of how users get pulled into your website's marketing strategy. The top of the funnel represents the broad awareness phase where you need to teach prospects you exist, and through a series of planned steps, they fall deeper and deeper until they eventually convert at the bottom of the funnel. By convert I mean they perform an intended goal such as a purchase or fill their data in a form.

Conversion marketing is legit. I have nothing against the strategy, but I feel that it only represents one half of the entire equation. Digital marketing allows us to go beyond one linear pass of the sales cycle. In fact, just as a cycle indicates, the digital marketing process is revolving. Metaphorically, the funnel is exactly the opposite of that – in and out. I'm proposing here that the user journey in a modern sales acquisition cycle is more representative of an infinite loop ∞ and not a funnel. A typical prospect does enter your acquisition cycle through wide-based awareness building. With the help of remarketing tactics, a prospect and client can fall deeper and deeper into your *"marketing hypnosis"* with every pass they take along the loop.

I find it interesting that in a Tarot deck, the infinite loop is represented on The Magician or Juggler card. One might think of an excellent marketing campaign as almost magic while poor marketing strategy can easily make your campaign a big joke. This model is no joke; rather, it's a way for you to build more clarity into the future. The Digital Acquisition Cycle (DAC Model) is a feedback tool, similar to the OODA Loop by the United States Air Force Col. John Boyd. The OODA is an acronym for Observe, Orient, Decide, and Act. It is used to examine decisions regarding military combat operations and applies to the human decision-making process. The OODA Loop outlines that we first observe the situation at hand. Then we orient ourselves to this situation based on our past experiences and any prior knowledge. Our decision, which leads to decisive action, is thus based on our known experiences, and each action creates a loop of constant feedback. In the military, this could constitute sending troops into the battle zone or retreating. In digital marketing, we can use the feedback loop to decide to stop what we're doing or double down. To make these types of educated guesses, we need a roadmap to determine our key performance indicators and the actions in between. That is what the DAC Model provides: a roadmap with spots for key performance validation, so you know that whatever you're doing, you're keeping your users on task and maximizing your marketing efforts. This will help reduce risk and maximize your opportunity with blogging and content marketing.

Let's look at the DAC Model and start to conceptualize the entire journey of a user.

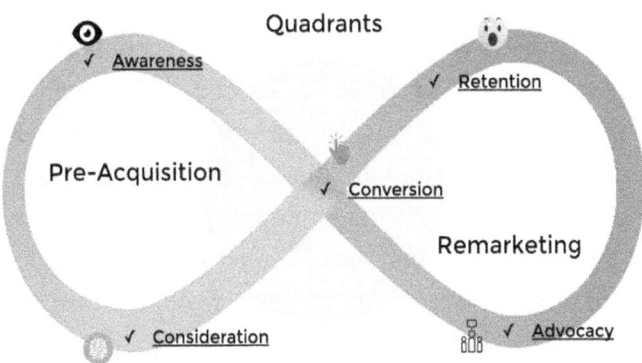

The DAC Model is broken into 5 main quadrants: the pre-acquisition phase, consideration, conversion zone, remarketing, and advocacy. Users travel through each one of these phases along the acquisition journey, almost like it's a racetrack with cars zooming along. A user will make a conversion touchpoint around each loop where they are intended to make some type of interaction with you or your content. Let's start at the beginning of the user journey.

Pre-Acquisition Phase

This left half of this loop represents the wide awareness phase. At this point, a prospect is cold, and we haven't yet made a touchpoint or introduction. The client might not even be aware we exist yet and is not yet in the race or on your racetrack. This half of the infinite loop represents tactics like advertising, marketing, PR, and digital strategy to make that initial impression and introduce our offer to our prospect through our website and digital marketing efforts. Advertising, marketing, and PR will generate awareness and get people into the race as they come to your website and aim for your goal. Users start at pre-acquisition and travel through consideration, where they will consume your ads and content to develop that initial awareness and trust level, which drives them closer to your offering. They are not fully acquired until after they make a conversion.

Conversion

This is where you go from the unknown to the known. Once a prospect is made aware you exist, through advertising, marketing, and PR, it's your goal that the prospect follows your funnel to your website. They need to make their way to your offer and convert into a lead. At that moment, they are no longer an unknown cold prospect but have converted into being a bona fide user. This sends them across the loop's figure 8 crossing and into the warm leads section. Here they will receive new types of marketing communication from you since they are now within your database.

Remarketing Phase

The remarketing phase is unique to digital marketing. Once we have a user's contact information, such as an email address they entered on a contact form or through a subscription to opt-in, they are now on the right half, or warm leads section, of the loop. We can then deploy remarketing tactics with various tools such as email marketing, content, and other tools to keep the user in the race and back around to make a second conversion. Thus we get either a larger sale or an advocate on our behalf who will refer us to a friend.

A well-tuned system will draw a user through this infinite loop several times, making multiple conversions into a variety of product and services, increasing the overall lifetime value of your marketing efforts. What we want to avoid are users falling off due to a *"leaking loop"* where they are either not the right customer to fit the product, or worse, your model is not fully optimized. Let's examine each phase of the Digital Acquisition Cycle in more detail, from the users' start to finish.

Pre-Acquisition Phase – The beginning

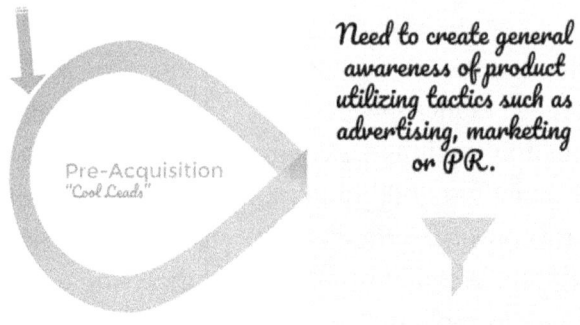

This is the first phase of the Digital Acquisition Cycle: building awareness

How do we reach someone who doesn't know we exist?

Unless you live under a rock, advertising, marketing, and public relations are all around you.

I'm sure you can think of some of your favorite jingles and slogans right now. Here in Chicago, there was a television ad campaign that started in the late '80s, and if you start to sing 588-2300...well then, almost anyone above the age of 30 in the greater Chicagoland area can finish the phone number for Empire Carpet. Catchy jingles, intriguing infomercials, and pop culture product placements, this is how advertising was done for so many years. There's no doubt that over the last several decades, advertising, marketing, and public relations has evolved. The tactics and strategies of generations before us wouldn't necessarily work today, would they?

Legendary inventor and T.V. pitchman, Ron Popeil, harnessed the airwaves to pitch his products for decades. With dozens of successful product launches, including the iconic Chop-O-Matic, the Popeil Pocket Fisherman, and later on products like the Showtime Rotisserie and BBQ, Popeil and his products became a household name. He essentially launched it all with a 5 minute long black and white commercial created for a little over $500 and a trademark simile. But wait, there's more! If you were to ask Popeil if he would do the same thing if he were to start from scratch today, well then, I'd guess his answer would ultimately be yes. The hustle and grit necessary to get any type of product off the ground is a core requirement. Target your consumers on the platforms where they consume the most content so we can demonstrate value is still a must.

For prior generations, this was the 30-second television and radio commercials during segmented periods such as prime-time, drive-time or day-time slots. Newspapers and print magazines were also kings of the ad biz industry as we flocked to trusted sources every day for a dose of world news, business, sports, and more. For the children of the baby boomer generation, the Millennials, and frankly most of the world today, consumption happens on social networks accessed on pocket-sized mobile devices. While the mediums have changed, the message has not. Our job, as a marketer, is to create compelling stories and distribute them to whoever is willing to consume them. Popeil would still need to make his infomercials, but they might air on Facebook versus cable TV.

Another example that comes to mind is celebrity TV Shark, inventor, and *"Queen of QVC"* Lori Greiner. Followed a similar path as Ron Popeil, Greiner hustled her jewelry cases to local department stores and would break out on a new TV network at the time called QVC – a home shopping channel where viewers would call in to place orders. Today, Greiner is a household influencer due to her roles on the popular television show Shark Tank and QVC. On the prime-time show, Grainer makes investments into startup business that come to pitch their offering. To date, Greiner has invested in some of the most profitable products in the show's history.

Greiner shares her full story in a fantastic, inspiring and bestselling book called *"Invent it, Sell it, Bank it..."* that's available on amazon.com. She explains how she hustled jewelry cases to get valuable feedback on her product. This feedback included how much a customer might be willing to pay for it, and was an important part of her journey to success. I wasn't there, but I can guess that she was targeting her ideal customers: women who would use the product, but were also open-minded enough to receive feedback from anyone who would take the time. Be sure to read the full story in her book.

I put these two American dream examples in this book because they represent exactly what you need to consider when building a blog and online platform today. You are the pitch-person for your product and content because it's only up to you to get your offering in front of eyeballs and into your consumer's head. Both Popeil and Greiner didn't wish for success or expect any platform to help them; they went out and made success using the resources they had at the time, and that created awareness for their products.

If you can get to your consumer so they can think *"Hey, I need this product, therefore, I will buy it,"* or *"Hey, I like this author. Therefore, I will subscribe to get more of their content,"* then you have created magic. This is what you need to sell and grow your blog and your authority online. Your advertising, marketing, and product development happen in the space between our prospects' ears and eyes. This has not changed in over a century and likely never will. Listen to your customers and get feedback on product fit. In order to do that, you must first go wider than normal and ask anyone who listens to give feedback. Know that everyone might not be a perfect fit. But if you start to hear the same feedback over and over, then it might be you.

That is sort of what you have to do with digital marketing. We go wide, get feedback from any users who are willing to click your ad, and then start to dial into the right users who are the likeliest to become customers. Once we have a handful of customers, then it's time to start to build the content and products the they actually want. How we deliver content and offers for consumers to ponder, now that has evolved. What was once dominated by print, radio and television ads is now joined by power players like Facebook and Google. Like any advertising medium, some are more effective than others, depending on your overall budget, goals, and target audience.

The platforms have changed, opening up a new, more affordable barrier of entry. It's still relatively the same bag of tricks that Empire Carpet, Ron Popeil and Lori Greiner used in the 1990s. The key is to provide perceived high-level value to your consumer, enough that they want to give up their hard earned money in exchange for a sale. To do this, you must first get your offering in front of as many eyeballs and into their minds as often as possible. I don't care if that is with social media advertising, Google Ads, email marketing, radio ads, expressway billboards, networking events with a business card or anywhere else your brand can show up to say hello. You must make a splash in front of anyone who will turn their head.

The real difference for bloggers today versus someone like Mr. Popeil is that your prospects will likely go to your website to learn more and make the transaction. Prospects are searching for you to validate your existence, and your website is the center of your strategy. Your website is also where the magic happens as users consume your content. It's where your advertising, branding, content, marketing, publicity, and the like, translate into your business' most important objective: the conversion.

Where Does Blogging Fit into Pre-Acquisition?

Blogging is a key driver of advertising and marketing for content-centric business, especially web-based apps and startup business with little known brand recognition. Blogging provides a relatively low-cost entry, and it is an excellent platform to showcase your values and your ideas to anyone who will listen.

Blogging, when done right and in enough quantity, can drive free traffic to your website through organic search engine optimization and social media sharing. This is ideal because you are generating clients with few advertising costs and that will contribute to a higher margin and more money in your pocket. There's a theory in digital marketing that most users will not actually come to your website or make a decision about exploring your product further after approximately 7 different asks.

This is the basis behind the existence of remarketing or retargeting. Your user might be scrolling their Facebook news feed and see your ad once. They might not do anything the first or second times, but after the third time, something may trigger them to click your website link to explore more.

Content and a well-executed blog can generate many touch points. A user might read four or five different posts before they start to build confidence in you or your brand. Creating a library of content will allow you to create multiple opportunities for prospects to review your content, so they click a headline that is most intriguing to them. Blog posts also need to be search engine friendly as they can be crafted in a way that answers a user question, tells an interesting story or narrates a relatable point of view. If you're able to create the right type of content, search engine traffic can create a great source of referral traffic that can fill your DAC Model for years.

Many factors go into search engine optimization (SEO), but blogging and creating content are always a good way to start. Being on the front line of publishing content will provide you valuable feedback to learn if your content is even SEO worthy. I consider myself lucky with a website and

SEO strategy that I deployed several years ago. I was able to rank in the number 1 spot for several organic search results related to my WordPress classes in Chicago. This placement provided me with years of high-quality referral traffic, and I was able to convert many of those visitors into paid workshop attendees. The beauty of it was I paid little to almost nothing to generate thousands of dollars for this side business.

Today I rely on a mix of organic search content and paid ads. It creates a more reliable influx of users, and since I have a budget to work with, I can focus on generating ROI positive campaigns.

Search engine optimization is a long term strategy. It can take months to years before you see any traffic on a particular targeted query if any traffic at all. My best advice is to create content for search, but also test as many advertising platforms as you can afford. Start with Facebook Ads, Google Ads, or other similar web platforms. At the end of this book, I've outlined an advertising plan based on your budget. You probably don't want to buy an expensive billboard on the highway just yet. Test on platforms that are the lowest cost to get into and you can easily turn it off if you need to make a change. I recommend starting with simply boosting a Facebook Ad of either a blog post you recently published or maybe even a local event that you can host.

This type of entry-level, low-cost advertising to test market fit is something I bet Ron Popeil could only wish he could have had access decades ago – maybe before he launched the Percolator, a combination coffee pot steam iron, one of the few products of his that flopped. Launching a new product before the digital marketing age involved a huge risk. The product would first have to be developed, possibly manufactured and stored in warehouses awaiting sales. Then, marketing and advertising agencies would create jingles and run TV, print, and radio ads. After all of that money was shelled out on the line, the market would tell you if it was a good investment or not.

Once you created and bought a TV ad, it's paid for whether your product is good or not. Digital marketing is way more flexible. You can adjust and test ads as you receive almost immediate feedback from website data and sales reports, even to the point where you can presell items to see if there is even a demand for interest in your product offering. At this point, if you're like me, you might be ready to jump into doing some ads. Don't! I highly recommend to not start any type of paid advertising until after you have a baseline DAC Model cobbled into place. For example, have a website, some initial product, and an offer tested with a small beta audience, maybe with your friends and family.

This is also a scary point because you must have full faith that your product and strategy are worth it, so much so that you're willing to put your hard earned money into ads to promote it. If you're not willing to spend money advertising it, then will your prospects willing to pay for it?

Be ready and willing to make a calculated risk. You might need to burn a bit of your advertising budget to get that valuable feedback from users. This is a scary point because you are putting yourself out into the world and opening yourself up for critical feedback. It was hard for me in the beginning, and it is still is at some level. You must get out of your comfort zone. I try not to cringe at 1-star reviews or nasty comment trolls. In fact, I thank them for giving me the feedback I need to make a better product that people are willing to spend their hard earned money on. I know that you can't win everyone over; it's just impossible. What is worse is not getting any feedback and spending thousands of dollars and hours on a dud of a product, or doing nothing at all.

Your Website

Author note: I use the term website and blog interchangeably.

Where do you send them on your website? You go from the first impression to a new subscriber. X marks the spot, like a treasure map. In the DAC Model, the crossing of figure eight is the treasure zone. This is where you, your prospect, and your goals all come together to create a touch point and hopefully, conversion. A touch point for the user can be as simple as a user entering their email address into your website to subscribe for updates or clicking the like button on your Facebook brand page. A touchpoint could be more complex, such as full-on product purchase or service appointment. Sometimes touchpoints have no physical connection, but rather a nebulous mental shift regarding a cause or ideal. At this point, at the center, you are the closest to your customer as they loop around the DAC Model and transition from the unknown into a user, follower, or supporter.

In the pre-acquisition phase, our focus was on advertising, marketing, and PR activities that established an initial awareness of our offering, that we even exist in this world. The goal was to just get prospects to your website and begin the consumption process. In the conversion zone, the goal is to take that unknown – the visitors that we attracted with our pre-acquisition efforts – and convert them into a known user. You may not be best friends just yet, but at some level, you can now identify that user with some type of data, such as an email address from a contact form submission.

The data you collect at the conversion touchpoint will depend on your campaign's objectives. The problem is it can be hard to get a prospect to gladly hand over their email address or credit card information. This level of comfort and trust requires a rather complex recipe of high-quality content, persuasive copy, and savvy marketing promotions. When mixed together correctly, it can create the lead generation machine you need to sustain your efforts as a blogger and marketer. Let's dive into exactly how to funnel users from the pre-acquisition phase and into their first conversion. Getting your prospects to X marks the spot. A website conversion strategy is kind of like treasure hunting. Except you created the map and your prospects are the treasure seekers. You are trying to steer your prospects down a path where they will find the location on their own. Except we're not trying to bury the treasure; we want it to be in clear sight so our hunters can easily find it.

How you design your treasure map or place your offer within your blog is up to you. There really isn't a right or wrong way to place your offer. Well, there is a wrong way: one where you don't get found. Just don't do that!

What's An Offer?

Somewhere within our site, we will need to literally provide the benefits and features of our products offer. Sometimes we're able to get away with just a graphic of a digital book. For more complex or high ticket products, we may need a video to do the job. The offer is a summary of what exactly the user can expect if they purchase or opt-in to our offer. How we get that offer in front of our prospects is where things get tricky. Conversion marketers utilize a toolbox of popups, visual cues, and other annoying tricks to funnel users further to the main offer page. Personally, I don't want to tell you to use web page pop-ups because they are annoying. But the reality is, they often work. And work well. I prefer pop-ups that don't appear until a user starts to leave the page. This is called exit intent, and it tracks the mouse position to see if they are reaching for the navigation bar to open a new tab or leave the page. This can help you from losing a prospect if they haven't actually made it the touch point zone. For a complete bag of conversion marketing tools and tricks, visit my website at blogyouwant.com/dac-resources.

Offer pages within your website might be a bit different than other pages. An ideal offer page creates a very directed experience with all of the content required to tell the story and draw users to a call to action. These were sometimes called squeeze pages, where we would squeeze a user into becoming a lead. I don't like this term; it sounds kind of shady, but it's partially true. I've been building websites and blogs for many years, so for me, it's pretty easy to create an entire website around an offer, but it doesn't necessarily have to be that complex. All you really need is one portion of your website to have a compelling story that will get users to act.

Case in point: in the fall of 2018, I created an opt-in campaign to promote my Creative Year Ever!™ workshop and workbook. My idea for Creative Year Ever! is to help others realize their most creative self and build a solid foundation for making the next year their most creative yet. My objective for this campaign was two-fold. Firstly, I wanted to validate if this product concept was something people wanted. Secondly, if it was a good idea, I wanted to collect email addresses to build a remarketing list for products and events within this brand. So far, so good. The user feedback I collected from the data I received turned out positive, providing me with direction on how I planned to carry out Creative Year Ever! in the future. Plus, I've collected email addresses to promote future content, products, and events.

I decided to create an entire website around this brand, but I could have just created one page within an existing website or blog to validate this idea a well. Given that I was able to register the domain name, creativeyearever.com, I decided to build out a small website with WordPress. I felt this was the best course of action for what I was trying to do. For a complete guide for registering domain names and working with WordPress, visit blogyouwant.com/dac-resources. The key component to the Creative Year Ever! campaign was probably not the website, but rather the inexpensive yet highly valuable lead magnet. A lead magnet is a tool we use to create an attractive offer, such as a free eBook download, where a user exchanges their contact information – in this case, an email address - for my gated, member-only content. There are plenty of lead generation ideas, an eBook is only one example.

Worksheets, cheat sheets, quizzes and courses are some others, to name a few. Users entered their email address, and within a few minutes, the eBook was delivered to their email via a MailChimp automation campaign. The user gets the information I promised, and I collect their email address for future mailings. A win-win, I say! Another example of landing pages conversion strategy that I have created is for my podcast website, the BlogYouWant.com. This is the always available and evergreen 7-Day Blogging Challenge, meaning it doesn't change very often. I plug this offer on each episode on my podcast, or at least I do when it makes sense, and ask listeners to enter the challenge and receive my special content via email. At the end of the email drip sequence, after I've sent 7 emails of high-quality content, I offer a promotion for my blog coaching services. Some users don't finish, and that's ok.

Others contact me to see how I can continue to help them past the 7 days. My goal with the podcast is to drive as many users to my landing page, and subsequent offer, so I can generate some business and help sustain my content marketing efforts. The 7-Day Blogging Challenge offer page is a bit different than the rest. If you visit the page https://blogyouwant.com/blogging-challenge/, you might notice that users can't access the rest of the website or any of my social media profiles. The only way one can receive the free email course is if they enter the main call to action with your name and email address.

My goal with this page is to create a very clear and direct call to action provided the user has very limited options. Adding social media or links to other blog posts might distract or detour my users from my primary conversion goal. If a user lands on this page, they do so after a lot of time and investment is spent on creating content or advertising. I don't want to lose the sale before I at least collect their email address. Of course, a visitor can use the browser back button or close the tab - I can't control that.

What's most important in this phase, and why we create special landing pages and lead magnets, is that we're trying to get the user to accelerate their consideration. We want our website visitors to think, *"That sounds like something I need and want."* Therefore, I will give you my email address, money, data, or whatever will help us market to them again in the future. For this to happen, we have to drive consideration, which is something that happens in our users' minds and not on the web page.

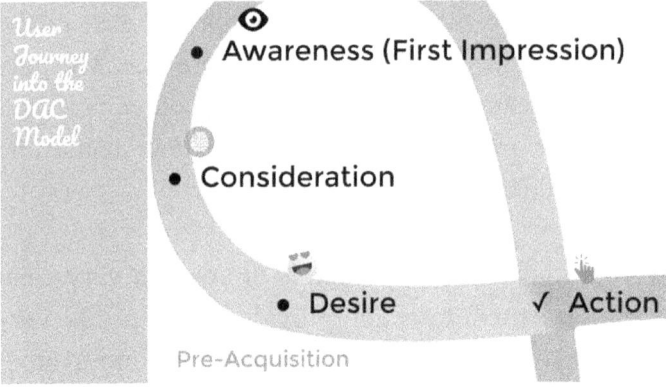

Consideration

Consideration is a tricky thing to optimize; it's not something that we as marketers really have control over. Rather, we can only do our best to be as persuasive as we can, in a matter of milliseconds. This is where old fashion marketing and offer promotions come into play. It's stuff the *"mad men"* of marketing used for years. We need to pull at the heartstrings of our users and get them to see a better life with our product or service. The delivery method we use to tell our story has changed, but we're still the same humans making the same decisions based on need and desire.

As soon as your prospects see your product offer, they will begin to engage in thoughtful tug-of-war deciding whether or not to buy now or to opt-in. For years, we focus a lot on optimizing websites for search, social, speed, and other more technical aspects but truly the most important optimization is for users' consideration. Humans are storytellers. We enjoy watching and consuming stories that we can relate to. These stories can also help sell a product with strategic messaging and other buyer validation signals. They create that emotional bond with a like-minded user that creates the bandwagon effect.

The behavioral science around marketing and selling is nothing new; most big brand products go through a series of *"marketing science"* and product engineering before they ever hit the shelves. Like most things, even these tactics can be flawed. Global brands spend big money on focus groups and market reports to still launch a flop. How can we forget the classic failures of New Coke and Crystal Clear Pepsi, the Apple Newton PDA, and more recently, Google+, the search engine giant's second attempt at a social network. These are just some of the many failed product launches that are only good today as the brunt of jokes.

Focus groups, color theory, product placement comparisons, and other triggers help scientists, marketers, and economists guess what will make consumers pull the trigger and buy their product or service over the competition. Today, this marketing science is translating into thoughtful web design and development. Some of the biggest brands today, such as Amazon.com, eBay.com, Google.com, and Facebook.com, are web-first businesses. You may not even realize it as a consumer, but many of these e-commerce businesses use a form of conversion testing on you every day. Split testing shows a small group of users' one version of a web page, while another group gets a completely different version.

After users browse in real time, data is collected to see which page performed better. The higher performing page stays and is tested against a new page to go through the process yet again. Subtle changes from tweaking a font size, or changing the color of a button can cause significant increases, or decrease, in sales and engagement. You'll only really know how users will interact when you get some real users to act. The science behind website optimization is a fascinating field that is growing in popularity with some of the biggest academic institutions across the globe.

The web has become the place for big business, and the research tends to follow the money. I know my limits, and I cannot speak at a very high level when it comes to the behavioral psychology of web design or behavioral economics, but I will share some of my own unscientific thoughts. When it comes to your offer, it's best to really dive in and consider how the story, price, supportive copy, design and other multimedia around your product's landing page can affect your prospects' decision-making process.

What is the overall value proposition of your offer?

For a visitor to your website, who is just learning about your offer, what is that most important point for them to take away?

Would you want this product?

If the answer is no to any of the above, then you might want to go back to the drawing board before you spend a ton of money on ads or marketing. Web page design plays a critical role in our prospects' decision process. This is why finding the right designer, copywriter, and developer is well worth it in the long run. Anyone can build a website. There are plenty of free to low-cost tools that let you make a website. It's the strategy behind the brand, design, and user experience that will foster consideration and drive sales, just like it has for centuries.

If you're on a budget, here are some thoughts to consider. When I sit down to design a landing page or any product, I try to put myself the best I can in my prospects' shoes.

What would the customer really want?

Are they looking for an explanation of a process, or are they looking for something to eliminate a process?

What can I do to eliminate any barriers, mental or physical, the prospect might be experiencing while considering my offer? What is my competition, and how are they doing it?

If you remember nothing else from this book, I hope that I can instill the concept of thinking as a user thinks. This is the only way to create something that people want. Then use feedback to pivot your product or marketing to become a perfect fit. It always comes down to product fit. You can have the best website in the world, but if your product is flawed, then your website marketing is doomed. Sometimes it is a simple as asking yourself, would I want and use this product at that price, and is this offer make a logical and compelling point? Your job as a marketer is to get your prospects to see it for themselves. You want your prospects to see a better life for themselves because they are using your product or information. That's why get rich quick schemes do so well. People often desire more money and a better life working at the beach. They can see themselves with more money and are looking for a quick fix to fill their desires.

I don't condone 'get rich quick' schemes – I'm just using them as an example. These types of schemes victimize and prey on unsuspecting users and offer little to no tangible results – sometimes through outright lies. How the users fall for these schemes is what I'm trying to explain here. They buy into the product because they are sold on the idea of a better life provided by the benefits of the product. This is a powerful concept that most marketers forget. You must sell the benefits, not the features. The field of psychology and behavioral science is ever evolving, and a lot of great information is coming online. That is why I created a free resource page with some of the top resources, new ideas, and books in the industry. Visit blogyouwant.com/dac-resources.

Designing Your Offer Pages

An offer page could be a home page of a site, but sometimes it's a specific page for a product offering. In some scenarios, landing pages do not include the site-wide navigation elements like the rest of the pages. This is because we don't want visitors to navigate away after we've perhaps paid to get them here. I avoid putting anything on this page that might distract a user from converting, such as social media profile links - unless that is your conversion objective of course.

I can't tell you exactly how you should design and optimize your landing pages because it's rather specific to your goals. High performing pages often incorporate many forms of media, including video, images, and copy that support the users' ability to see themselves with your product. Plus, if there was a one size fits all model, I wouldn't need to write this book. What often does work well are testimonials, money-backed guarantees, and other pre-sale help resources that can put the prospect at ease while they make a decision. Just try to limit your barrier of entry. If you're creating an opt-in form, try to limit the number of required fields or questions your user must answer in order to submit the form. They may be willing to share their first name and email address but start asking about their annual household income, and it could cause them to run away. Your overall trust with the prospect plays a big role in the buyer decision process. This is one reason why content marketing is key for selling online. If prospects already have a level of built-in trust by consuming your content, then they are likely more willing to purchase a product from you. It will require less selling to make that happen. The more known your brand becomes, the more at ease your prospects will be with your offers so you can get away with asking more details before they convert.

More *"cold"* prospects that come to your landing page, perhaps from a Facebook or Instagram Ad, might need more selling on the landing page or in the actual ad. It depends on the setup, but go and test ideas to see what landing page conversion techniques work best for you and your offering. A user is probably not going to buy a high ticket item in a popup, but they may download a low-cost presale offer or initiate a live chat module. Just make sure that you are working the pre-acquisition phase to get as many eyeballs on your offer as possible, and be prepared to make changes to your landing page conversion strategy as you receive live user data.

As you browse the web, start to notice the offer pages and see what worked to convert you and what didn't work. If you click on a Facebook ad, notice where it takes you. Try to see if you can easily leave that page; it's like being in a casino, the way they make it hard by design to find the exit. I suggest doing a Google Image Search for offer page ideas/designs, and you will find countless images of landing pages. I have also created a free landing page swipe file that you can download as a start. Go to this book's resources page at blogyouwant.com/dac-resources and find some recommended sources for offer and landing page inspiration with some up to date case studies.

Remarketing: The Second Half of DAC Model

Now that we got 'em, what do we do with 'em?

I think a lot of people who call themselves marketers today forget that they are not just trying to build followings online, post pictures and promote things. Yes, that's an important part of the process, but it's not the most important. If you are creating a blog and you plan to use the DAC Model to build a sustainable ecosystem around creating content, then you must also be ready to become a salesperson and sell your products.

Never forget this, the purpose of marketing is to support sales. Period. Marketing is a significant business expense - a calculated risk - and sales are how we recoup that cost.

Legendary management consultant, educator, and author Peter Drucker said, *"The purpose of a business is to create and keep a customer."* Prospecting for new clients or acquiring new leads is an important part of the process, but it's only one half of the process.

Working your existing database is essential to build a true growth strategy. Not to mention that it's much easier to sell to a previously satisfied customer.

Actively working your existing followers will help you generate more revenue, at a significantly reduced cost. It may cost you $60 to acquire a new customer after you factor in things like advertising, website investment, or labor. Upgrading existing customers might only cost $20 or less. These are just made up numbers for my example, but the bottom line is, your blog and business' growth depend on remarketing strategies to expand your customers overall lifetime value at a reduced cost. I know what you might be thinking. When I mention sales at my blogging workshops, I see a fearful look on people's faces.

People sometimes walk out at this point. I can just imagine what they are thinking. Sales to some is like a bad word that represents cold calling and hard selling tactics. I don't think they realized what they signed up for when they started blogging. Selling is something people try to avoid like the plague, myself included. Good news, you don't have to do anything super spammy - unless you want.

Remarketing is the process of using content and digital communication mediums as your selling vehicle, and in this section, we're going to discuss how we can really elevate your blog to the next level by cultivating your base. Now that we have delivered on our promises to our users and provided the offer they opted into or purchased, we have entered them into the remarketing phase. This puts us in a great situation. We have their trust, their data, and maybe even their money. Now, what are we going to do with it? The second half of the Digital Acquisition Cycle are the sales tactics we use to market to our known users. I refer to this as the remarketing phase.

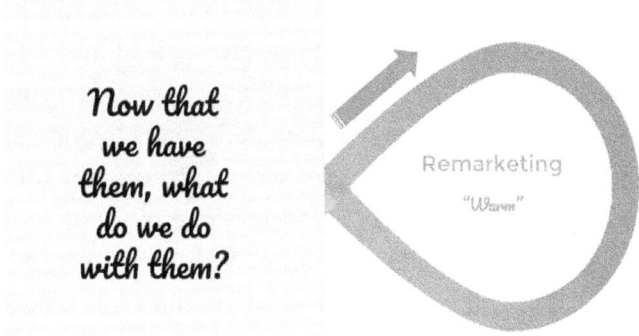

Now that we have them, what do we do with them?

Remarketing

"Warm"

The infinite loop has transitioned from blue into orange. In a traditional sales and marketing department, warm leads are the holy grail of sales. These are prospects that are ready to buy, and you are just the person to sell them what they need. Your content strategy, at this point, also reflects that. We're no longer talking to an unknown user but rather to a single person with a name and a data trail. Given all of the data points we may have collected, we can create and send personalized content that provides the maximum value to our users. Follow this up by a few touchpoints – or emails – to get them excited and interested in our next conversion goal.

For example, a user might make the first conversion by going to your blog and downloading a free or low-cost PDF lead magnet. They enter your email marketing campaign, and we send them a series of content that they actually want, based on the topics the book covers. We can use the lead magnet's theme to get an idea of the problem our user is trying to solve and then create automated emails to address those issues over a series of weeks and months. For example, if an unknown user converts on a lead magnet to help them launch a WordPress website, then I have an idea of the content and pain points they might be facing based on the lead magnet. I will then create an email marketing campaign to send and address these points. The end goal is providing them a secondary product – may be a course or mastermind – they will want, given their new skills and information.

In addition to accelerating our prospect into our second conversion goal, we're also working them to help advocate on our behalf and bring in new users who will start their own journey into your Digital Acquisition Cycle (DAC). The beauty of blogging and content creation is that it's very sharable. We might simply ask them to share our existing content to their social media profiles or refer it to a friend. This is how we will get new users into our DAC Model without the cost of advertising. Out of the two halves of the DAC Model, the remarketing side is harder to maintain, but very powerful when executed correctly. User engagement skills and the willpower to persist with massive content creation are what successful content marketers do to build authority and sales online. A poorly executed remarketing campaign is like taking a firehose and puncturing a hole in it halfway. Advertising might provide a powerful stream of inbound pressure from the hydrant, but if there's a leak somewhere in the hose, your marketing efforts will lose pressure and the fire will rage on.

It is seemingly more attractive – ego stroking, even – to want to focus on acquiring new subscribers. Sometimes it can even be easier, depending on our budget or content production system. But focusing on pre-acquisition should not be at the expense of your remarketing efforts. We need users to make multiple conversions to both reduce your cost-per-acquisition numbers and increase the overall lifetime value of a user. Most importantly, we need your base to advocate for you and bring new users in by leveraging their own followers and friends. A recommendation from a friend or trusted colleague is priceless.

Wide advertising is a great tool, but my main focus is using content to create referrals through the viral sharing of content and word of mouth. Having someone share a blog post or video on LinkedIn is a million times more valuable than sponsoring a post on Facebook. Yes, we may need to sort of grease the wheels a bit with advertising to get some initial users in to our DAC Model, but it is our primary job to work our existing base of users and reduce your dependency on advertising. The number #1 tool you have for remarketing is something you probably use every day. Email, by far, is my favorite remarketing tool as it reaches the widest demographic and often checked the most often. I know what you're thinking.

I also get tons of promotional email every day from some of the most aggressive salespeople, marketers, and spammers.

Email as a communication tool is definitely ingrained into our society. Not only do I get thousands of promotional emails every day, but I also get a few nuggets of importance from my bosses, doctors, mechanics, schools, and everyone else I communicate with regularly. We tend to treat email more respectfully as a communication tool, and I believe that if you create the right type of content and become the person people want to hear from, email is your ticket. If your following wants to read your content, they will. I skim my inbox to find email promotions from the brands that I want to read. If you make yourself a desirable brand that people want, they will read it. This is only done by providing the most value you can to a target audience that wants it.

Not to discredit other communication tools such as chatbots and text messages - these mediums can get the job done. It's just that not a lot of people I know are into chatbots yet and I hold text messages even more sacred than emails. The bottom line to a successful remarketing campaign is to create content that people want to read and send it to them when they want it. Don't be that marketer who is too aggressive or forgotten because of lack of persistence. Send me an email every day, and you're probably more likely to get me to unsubscribe. Send me an email on Friday afternoons, and I might open it if I'm at my desk as I tend to reserve that time to *"catch up."* Send me emails promoting others' products without providing what I would expect from you, and I will start to lose that brand/trust connection with you.

It's up to you to learn and understand your audience and figure out their true needs and wants. What truly powers remarketing is the content. Email is the vehicle, but the content is the message. That's the beauty of being a content creator. You might already have a huge leg up on the remarketing side with your existing content. After someone converts into your email database, start an email campaign with links to your existing or new content. Use the OODA Loop for feedback, as explained at the beginning of this section, and continue to test and improve your content to find your highest value and converting content. The key is to design an email campaign that addresses users' wants and supplies them with content at the moment they need it. This takes trial and error to find the sweet spot and your never-ending quest to really understand your prospects.

The secondary conversion, the next goal we generate from remarketing, can be anything. It might be a higher ticket item like a mastermind course, workshop, or full book purchase. It could be asking for a 5-star review or a referral, but an ask should only come after you have done everything you can do delight your followers and help them reach their true potential. Remarketing is not always about automation. We use automation of emails and other tools because we're trying to scale and reach as many users at once. But you would be surprised what a personal email or thank you card can do you for you. If your customer just shelled out $2,000 for your master course, then you might want to follow up with them personally to meet and exceed their expectations. This might call for a personal email or even a personalized video.

This type of personalized service can help keep customers wanting more and grateful for their purchase. Not looking for a refund. These personalized touch points, where you really able to help someone break through their current state of affairs, is what helps shift users from just passively following you to becoming a source of referrals.

Sending your next client around the DAC Model just like the first one. Advocacy might not even be an obtrusive ask, but rather simple hacks that can help accelerate user referrals. For example, it could be an affiliate program where you offer your existing following a small bonus, gift, or private group membership for referring people to you.

One of the best referral *"growth hacking"* programs on the planet was Dropbox, the service that offered free space to every user you referred to their app. Similar referral hacks include Gmail and Pinterest, which both started as member-only platforms where users had a limited number of invites they could use for their friends. These are great examples of how your product can work on your behalf to create referrals, so new users fall into your DAC Model to keep a sustainable ecosystem of new users and remarketing to users you already have. This will help you reduce your dependence on advertising and increase your word of mouth marketing. The challenge comes when you're trying to scale your efforts and grow beyond only a few hundred to maybe a few thousand users. Scale brings new problems, but being on the front line can help you come up with creative solutions to fix problems

Putting it all together:

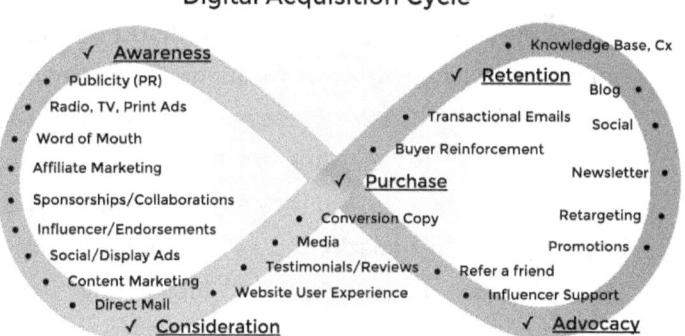

Digital Acquisition Cycle™

Remarketing Like In the Ads Platform?

Remarketing may ring a bell if you've dabbled in this space for a while. In digital ads, there are remarketing display ads. This tool allows you to show ads to users who have already visited your website or a certain page. It's a powerful tool and can be part of my remarketing process, but I have a bit of a different take. Remarketing in the DAC Model relates to activities content marketers engage in with the intent of capturing the attention of users already aware of your existence. This can be in the form of email marketing, social media posts, or any type of distributed content where users follow your brand.

I want to be clear – the term remarketing is not something that I coined. It's actually a term inspired by remarketing tools in popular Ads platforms. These remarketing ad tools are similar to how I use the term remarketing, but they are not completely the same. I think of remarketing as the bigger picture. I agree that you must reach a user many times before they make a conversion. In the DAC Model, remarketing is simply the process of reaching out to existing customers or subscribers with the objective of pulling users closer to an intended conversion.

Remarketing is about providing the most value, leveraging your content to share your expertise and maximizing your engagement with your following so you can grow your sphere of influence and sell more product and get more referrals.

Sending Users Around And Around

Complete Customer Journey

The DAC Stacked

Each time a user laps around the loop, it's like they have reached a turbo boost. At that point, after they just completed a conversion touch point and you've provided them something of value, they are their most primed to want to help you or buy more from you. It's sort of like the merry-go-round in a children's playground. The merry-go-round will spin but eventually lose momentum if someone is not on the outside, spinning it around. You are that person; you need to keep spinning your users around and around. The DAC Model is an infinite loop by design. The concept of sending prospects and known users around and around in a two-step conversion cycle is what I want to convey to you the most with this book. You must not stop after the first conversion. If you wish to truly grow your authority online and benefit from content marketing, then you must pay close attention to your users' complete journey now and into the future. Once you've mastered the first two-step conversion, then begin to look into how you can stack new conversions on top of your first two. An infinite loop is exactly that – it never ends. You can essentially use your base users to market an unlimited number of conversions if you have the products and content to keep your base warm and engaged. This essentially creates a system that pulls users deeper into your platform and allows you to generate more revenue to sustain your marketing acquisition costs. Let's say that conversion one is an email opt-in where we obtain a user's email address. Once we have them in our list, we send them a series of automated drip emails that help build rapport, and ultimately sell them a digital good – let's say an online course. That would be a great example of a two-step model.

Now, what happens after they finish the course?

It doesn't have to end there. We could funnel users into a new conversion - maybe another more advanced course. Or we ask them to subscribe to a podcast or ask for a referral. We just need to keep an eye on where prospects are at within our DAC Model and look at what their next goal is and how we can get them to it. This is where customer relationship management tools (CRM) come into use, as they can provide a dashboard to track your users along their journey from prospect and beyond. The DAC Model is a powerful strategy that provides flexibility for different types of goals. If you think about it, most conversions for your business follow a similar model. Here are some examples of two-step conversions that fit into a DAC Model cycle. User lands on your website, leaves, but comes back and converts with Google Ads Remarketing or Facebook Retargeting to then purchase your book.

Search user navigates your blog post; converts into a newsletter subscriber. Remarketing drip email persuades them to buy course within 60 days.

A user finds your product through a targeted Facebook ad, makes a purchase, and follows your Facebook page. The user then makes a second purchase because of a Facebook post of a second product, then refers friends by tagging product in the story.

A user installs your app with Facebook Ads, becomes an annual pro member in 15 days after trial and with promo code sent from email marketing campaign to new users.

A prospect learns about your business in a trade publication, visits your website and enquires about the product with contact form. Sale made in 60 days from a drip email sequence.

User lands on a blog from search; leaves a positive comment, and shares post to Twitter.

Prospect sees a billboard for your service, calls to book an appointment. Follow up email sequence converts into leaving a 5-star review.

In conclusion:

The DAC Model is a plan that, when executed correctly, can create extraordinary results. You will experience pitfalls and problems along your journey. That is why having a clear understanding of your purpose will help you remember why you are doing what you're doing. It will be hard, and you will make mistakes. That's ok! We're here to help. Be sure to join our community of DACers at blogyouwant.com/dac-resources. Share your questions and hear from others who are in your shoes and what is working – or not working – for them. Just know that with proper management of your marketing strategy, your success will come. Persistence, knowledge, and the desire to win are the traits of a successful player of this game.

Start small, learn that only good comes from failure, and make the time to truly live out your digital strategy. I want to leave you with inspiration from one of my business idols, Dick Portillo, the founder of the famous Chicago-based restaurant chain. Mr. Portillo didn't grow a billion dollar payout overnight, as he sold his restaurant chain in 2014. For legendary founder and entrepreneur Dick Portillo, it took decades of perfecting Portillo's strategy. As he outlined in his book, *Out of the Dog House: Turning a 1,100 investment into a Billion Dollar Profit*, it took many hard-knock lessons for him to figure out what his customers wanted.

And so he learned how to scale his offering with the right team, and fine-tune the customer experience to turn his restaurant operations into a restaurant empire. Portillo's success started with a one-man hot dog stand, where he showed up every day and began to build his fortune one dog at a time. Your digital marketing strategy is the same. It's the operations of your business, and it will take time and mistakes to realize your most profitable acquisition plan. When it starts to work, you will know why as the DAC Model has outlined a feedback model to follow. You will be prepared to scale your operations into more profitable opportunities for you and your organization when you actually start to get paid to do what you love. Don't blog for free, but also don't expect people to pay you for something they can't purchase. Test and build a product that people actually want, and then launch it to the world with your creative content. Most importantly, listen to your customers and team members. You are in the business to serve your customers, so let them tell you what they want and how they want it. Don't get stuck in your own ways; let them drive your marketing strategy as everything you do is for them.

Thank you for reading my book. If you have any questions, get in touch by going to blogyouwant.com/dac-resources. Please consider sharing this book with someone who will find value in it. Download the DAC Model Worksheet and PowerPoint Presentation at blogyouwant.com/dac-resources and join our community of DACers, other people who are living their journey and growing their visibility online.

The Digital Acquisition Cycle™ Worksheet

Key Goal (Metric)	Offerings to Consider	Offerings to Consider
Target Audience	Conversion Channel	Remarketing Activity & Channels
Pre Acquisition Activity & Channels		
	Remarketing Goal	Goal 2

Copyright © 2019 - Front & Social, LLC

Living in the DAC Model

A great racer, a great golfer or a great swimmer knows the entire course, every lap around the track, every bump in the road. They show up, practice often, and run trials just to continue to feel the course. That is how you should consider your digital marketing strategy. You must know the turns and the straightaways! There is simply no way your strategy will work if you are even slightly unaware of how you ought to take your digital strategy. There's this stigma that one must outsource all of their digital marketing as if someone else can do it better, faster than them and generate a lot more sales leads than them.

Honestly, after years of providing marketing consulting services, in my opinion, the more the primary beneficiary knows about their marketing strategy, the better their strategy will become. Sure, an agency that you outsource to is an expert in digital marketing, but they barely have an idea about your business industry. For instance, if your business belongs to medicine, then you would have a better understanding of your target audience as compared to the digital marketing agency that you outsource to. You will have to provide them with sufficient information to design your strategy in a way that seems appealing to your audience.

Ideally, the person who must be in the driver's seat is you or an in-house talent that is also dependent on your success. Unless you're hiring a consultant or a freelancer that can devote 100% of their time and energy to your strategy, you're setting yourself up for a huge risk. It's almost impossible for a solo freelancer to run your digital marketing course for multiple clients, mainly because marketing is such an important part of the business cycle. It's important for your marketer to know when sales are good, slow, and when to adjust. I understand why someone would want to outsource, especially if you're only one person in your business then there can be more efficient uses of your time, but for the most modern businesses, your marketing and sales is the most important aspect of your business. There just isn't anything better for you to do that you prioritize over that.

Digital marketing is a lot of work and involves several moving parts. Even if you feel like you can't cater to it by yourself and you need assistance with it, you shouldn't outsource it until you have run its complete course yourself at least once. If you don't care about your strategy and you want to waste money hiring out, then, by all means, be my guest.

However, if you want to be successful, instead of outsourcing, you must live in the DAC Model!

The DAC Model in Action!

In this model, the starting and finish line goals are ambiguous, but each lap around the loops represents a touchpoint bringing your prospects one step closer to your defined objective. This touchpoint could be sharing a piece of content, making a sale, referring a friend, or accepting your position. Around these loops, you have to maintain your pace, so racers within the loops complete the course and accelerate through the finish line to become true advocates of your brand.

Unfortunately, for various reasons, cars sometimes spin out of stall. Just like cars, the various factors in your digital marketing strategy can tend to go off track; therefore, it becomes your job to make sure that it doesn't happen within this race. The DAC Model has similarities to a traditional sales funnel, but what's different here is that I'm trying to build an entire marketing ecosystem and visualize what to do with your database of warm prospects, or clients, or followers once you have them into your platform.

This is where knowing the 'why,' the 'who,' and the 'what' as in earlier lessons, comes into critical play. Knowing them will bring focus on what your needs are to reach the people you want to make your potential and loyal customers.

You must take care of five points on this racetrack to maintain a successful strategy:
- Awareness of the starting line
- Consideration of U-turns
- Conversion of the straightaway clients
- The retention corner
- Using the advocacy underpass

Regardless of whether you have an entire sales team, or it's just you, when you're trying to build out your first outreach program, the DAC Model will help you identify what you must do with your prospects and how you can convert them from web traffic into digital leads to followers, and eventually into customers. In order to do that efficiently, we must understand how to use both general traffic and unique traffic to our advantage.

While getting the DAC Model into action, you must consider your lead flow. You have to do something to convert them into the DAC Model.

Once created, your DAC Model is an infinite cycle that not only keeps you in the race but also helps you win it. So, what's the next race for your customers? Wait for my next workbook to find out!

Here, I am going to help you in answering the following questions for your business through the DAC Model.

What am I trying to do here - get more followers or cultivate my existing base?

Where would an average user enter my DAC Model?

What would make them complete the first lap?

What is my conversion goal? How are we going to capture our prospects' data?

What are we going to do with it once we have it?

Expanded Anytime Questions:

- How effective is my current website? Can I incorporate a digital marketing campaign into what is existing or will I need to rethink?
- What would make a user more comfortable about entering their data/credit?
- What are my upsells?
- What tools will I use to build out the process?
- What will provide acceleration of users?
- What will slow users down?
- What are my tools to help my users make referrals?
- What types of devices are my users most likely using to consume my information?
- How will I measure the ROI of my DAC Campaign?
- How can I position my product to increase referrals? Can I offer any type of referral to a friend or affiliate promotion?
- Where might be my biggest pitfalls during the cycle? Where might I lose people?
- How will I ask users/prospects for their business? For their referrals? How direct will I be with my marketing efforts?
- Where am I currently winning?
- What pages and posts do your users visit most or the least?

- Where should they be visiting, and where are they not?
- How are we going to protect our customer's data?
- What are some no-cost or low-cost opportunities to reach your ideal audience base?

What to do when you have $20 - $500, $500 - $2000, $5000+ monthly budget

$20 - $500

- Use it to promote a local event or workshop on Facebook
- Boost some of your best content to drive traffic to your posts on social networks
- Boost a video shared to your business page on Facebook
- Dabble, test and repeat

$500 - $2K

- This is the danger zone; you don't quite have enough for the big leagues, and you're at a point where you could easily overspend if you don't have your DAC plan in place.
- First of all, determine how much education you need to explain what your product provides. If you have to overly educate users on why or how they

would use your product, then you might want to focus on *"top of funnel"* type techniques to build overall brand awareness such as promoting a video on Facebook. These ads are helpful for introducing your product/brand to prospective users, but they may or may not generate conversions.

- I would suggest looking into contextual advertising platforms such as Google Search Ads, to advertise to users who are looking for products similar to yours. At least you know they are looking for something you have to offer and can capture them during the need.

$5k or more

- You're on a launching platform for an ROI positive campaign. Use this budget to fine tune your DAC strategy and mix your ads into a blend of awareness building, remarketing, and conversion optimization strategy.

- Avoid spending money on services that *"help"* you if you can. If the service is just a fancy landing page, then create one on your website or hire a developer to build a landing page on your website and only pay once vs. a monthly fee that eats into your ad spend budget or overall profits. Invest in training so you can live your strategy.

- Remember, you can't just throw money at it and expect it all to work. Regardless of whether you have $50 bucks or $50k, you need to work the DAC strategy until it's finely tuned and operates on the lowest cost per acquisition as possible. Don't give up until you achieve this.

Thank you!

Thank you for reading this book, if you have any questions for feedback, please visit my resource pages at blogyouwant.com/dac-resources. I appreciate any feedback or stories of how this system is working, or not working, for you. Join me for live online instruction and at upcoming events, plus check out my podcast.

Please consider leaving a review for this book and share it with someone who would find value in it.